50 Bread Lover Dishes for Home

By: Kelly Johnson

Table of Contents

- Classic Garlic Bread
- Sourdough Grilled Cheese
- French Toast Casserole
- Cheesy Pull-Apart Bread
- Bruschetta with Tomato and Basil
- Monte Cristo Sandwich
- Bread Pudding with Vanilla Sauce
- Stuffed Italian Stromboli
- Cinnamon Swirl Bread
- Cheddar Jalapeño Cornbread
- Panzanella Salad
- Banana Nut Bread
- Baked Brie in a Bread Bowl
- Spinach and Feta Stuffed Flatbread
- Honey Butter Dinner Rolls
- Pumpkin Spice Bread
- Classic Reuben Sandwich
- Soft Pretzels with Mustard Dip
- Italian Focaccia with Rosemary
- Croque Monsieur
- Avocado Toast with Poached Egg
- Savory Herb and Cheese Biscuits
- Cuban Sandwich
- Sticky Toffee Bread Pudding
- New Orleans Beignets
- Classic Bagels with Cream Cheese
- Caramelized Onion and Gruyère Tart
- Turkish Pide with Ground Lamb
- Garlic Knots with Marinara
- Nutella-Stuffed Croissants
- German Soft Pretzel Rolls
- Challah French Toast
- Classic BLT Sandwich
- Spicy Buffalo Chicken Sliders
- Irish Soda Bread

- Ham and Cheese Croissant Sandwich
- Baguette with Olive Tapenade
- Cinnamon Raisin Bagels
- Spinach and Artichoke Dip with Bread Bowl
- Tomato and Mozzarella Panini
- Prosciutto and Fig Flatbread
- Texas Toast with Herb Butter
- Classic Philly Cheesesteak
- Chocolate Chip Banana Muffins
- Cornbread with Honey Butter
- Apple Cinnamon Bread
- French Baguette with Brie and Jam
- Meatball Sub Sandwich
- Olive and Parmesan Focaccia
- Cheesy Bacon Breadsticks

Classic Garlic Bread

Ingredients:

- 1 baguette
- ½ cup butter, melted
- 3 cloves garlic, minced
- 2 tbsp parsley, chopped
- ¼ cup Parmesan cheese (optional)

Instructions:

1. Preheat oven to 375°F (190°C).
2. Mix melted butter, garlic, and parsley in a bowl.
3. Slice the baguette lengthwise and brush with the butter mixture.
4. Sprinkle Parmesan if using.
5. Bake for 10-12 minutes until golden and crispy.

Sourdough Grilled Cheese

Ingredients:

- 2 slices sourdough bread
- 2 tbsp butter, softened
- ½ cup shredded cheddar cheese
- ½ cup shredded Gruyère cheese

Instructions:

1. Heat a skillet over medium heat.
2. Butter one side of each slice of bread.
3. Place cheese between slices with buttered sides facing outward.
4. Cook for 3-4 minutes on each side until golden brown and cheese melts.

French Toast Casserole

Ingredients:

- 1 loaf of bread, cubed
- 4 eggs
- 2 cups milk
- ½ cup heavy cream
- ½ cup sugar
- 1 tbsp vanilla extract
- 1 tsp cinnamon
- ¼ tsp nutmeg

Instructions:

1. Preheat oven to 350°F (175°C).
2. Grease a baking dish and place the bread cubes inside.
3. In a bowl, whisk eggs, milk, cream, sugar, vanilla, cinnamon, and nutmeg.
4. Pour the mixture over the bread and let soak for 30 minutes.
5. Bake for 40-45 minutes until golden and set.

Cheesy Pull-Apart Bread

Ingredients:

- 1 round loaf of bread
- ½ cup butter, melted
- 3 cloves garlic, minced
- 1 cup shredded mozzarella cheese
- ½ cup shredded Parmesan cheese
- 2 tbsp chopped parsley

Instructions:

1. Preheat oven to 375°F (190°C).
2. Cut the bread in a grid pattern without slicing all the way through.
3. Mix melted butter, garlic, and parsley.
4. Stuff the bread with cheese and drizzle with butter mixture.
5. Wrap in foil and bake for 20 minutes. Uncover and bake for 5 more minutes.

Bruschetta with Tomato and Basil

Ingredients:

- 1 baguette, sliced
- 3 tomatoes, diced
- ¼ cup fresh basil, chopped
- 2 cloves garlic, minced
- 2 tbsp olive oil
- 1 tbsp balsamic vinegar
- Salt and pepper to taste

Instructions:

1. Preheat oven to 400°F (200°C).
2. Toast baguette slices for 5-7 minutes until golden.
3. Mix tomatoes, basil, garlic, olive oil, balsamic vinegar, salt, and pepper.
4. Spoon the mixture over toasted bread and serve.

Monte Cristo Sandwich

Ingredients:

- 2 slices white bread
- 2 slices ham
- 2 slices turkey
- 2 slices Swiss cheese
- 1 egg
- ¼ cup milk
- 1 tbsp butter
- Powdered sugar (optional)

Instructions:

1. Assemble the sandwich with ham, turkey, and cheese between bread slices.
2. In a bowl, whisk egg and milk.
3. Dip the sandwich in the egg mixture, coating both sides.
4. Heat butter in a pan and cook the sandwich for 3-4 minutes on each side until golden.
5. Dust with powdered sugar if desired.

Bread Pudding with Vanilla Sauce

Ingredients:

- 4 cups cubed bread
- 2 cups milk
- 2 eggs
- ½ cup sugar
- 1 tsp vanilla extract
- ½ tsp cinnamon

For Vanilla Sauce:

- ½ cup heavy cream
- ¼ cup sugar
- 1 tsp vanilla extract

Instructions:

1. Preheat oven to 350°F (175°C).
2. In a bowl, whisk eggs, milk, sugar, vanilla, and cinnamon.
3. Pour over bread cubes and let soak for 30 minutes.
4. Bake for 40 minutes until set.
5. For the sauce, heat cream, sugar, and vanilla in a saucepan over low heat until thickened.
6. Drizzle over warm bread pudding before serving.

Stuffed Italian Stromboli

Ingredients:

- 1 pizza dough
- ½ cup marinara sauce
- 1 cup shredded mozzarella cheese
- ¼ cup Parmesan cheese
- ½ cup sliced pepperoni
- ½ cup cooked Italian sausage
- 1 egg, beaten

Instructions:

1. Preheat oven to 375°F (190°C).
2. Roll out pizza dough into a rectangle.
3. Spread marinara sauce and layer with cheese, pepperoni, and sausage.
4. Roll tightly and seal edges.
5. Brush with egg wash and bake for 25 minutes until golden brown.
6. Slice and serve.

Cinnamon Swirl Bread

Ingredients:

- 3 cups all-purpose flour
- 1 packet (2 ¼ tsp) yeast
- ¾ cup warm milk
- ¼ cup sugar
- 1 egg
- ¼ cup butter, melted
- ½ cup brown sugar
- 2 tbsp cinnamon

Instructions:

1. In a bowl, combine yeast, warm milk, and sugar. Let sit for 5 minutes.
2. Mix in egg, butter, and flour to form a dough. Knead for 8 minutes.
3. Let the dough rise for 1 hour.
4. Roll out dough, spread brown sugar and cinnamon evenly, then roll tightly.
5. Place in a greased loaf pan and let rise for another 30 minutes.
6. Bake at 350°F (175°C) for 35 minutes until golden brown.

Cheddar Jalapeño Cornbread

Ingredients:

- 1 cup cornmeal
- 1 cup all-purpose flour
- 1 tbsp baking powder
- ½ tsp salt
- 1 cup buttermilk
- 2 eggs
- ¼ cup melted butter
- 1 cup shredded cheddar cheese
- 1 jalapeño, diced

Instructions:

1. Preheat oven to 375°F (190°C) and grease a baking dish.
2. In a bowl, mix cornmeal, flour, baking powder, and salt.
3. In another bowl, whisk buttermilk, eggs, and melted butter.
4. Combine wet and dry ingredients, then fold in cheddar and jalapeño.
5. Pour into the baking dish and bake for 25 minutes until golden brown.

Panzanella Salad

Ingredients:

- 4 cups cubed stale bread
- 2 large tomatoes, diced
- ½ red onion, thinly sliced
- ½ cucumber, sliced
- ¼ cup basil leaves
- 3 tbsp olive oil
- 1 tbsp balsamic vinegar
- Salt and pepper to taste

Instructions:

1. Toast bread cubes in the oven at 350°F (175°C) for 10 minutes.
2. In a bowl, mix tomatoes, onion, cucumber, and basil.
3. Add toasted bread, drizzle with olive oil and balsamic vinegar, and season with salt and pepper.
4. Toss and let sit for 15 minutes before serving.

Banana Nut Bread

Ingredients:

- 2 ripe bananas, mashed
- ½ cup butter, melted
- ¾ cup sugar
- 2 eggs
- 1 tsp vanilla extract
- 1 ½ cups flour
- 1 tsp baking soda
- ½ tsp salt
- ½ cup chopped walnuts

Instructions:

1. Preheat oven to 350°F (175°C) and grease a loaf pan.
2. In a bowl, mix mashed bananas, butter, sugar, eggs, and vanilla.
3. In another bowl, whisk flour, baking soda, and salt.
4. Combine wet and dry ingredients, then fold in walnuts.
5. Pour into the loaf pan and bake for 50-55 minutes.

Baked Brie in a Bread Bowl

Ingredients:

- 1 round bread loaf
- 1 wheel of Brie cheese
- 2 tbsp honey
- ¼ cup chopped pecans
- 1 tbsp fresh rosemary

Instructions:

1. Preheat oven to 375°F (190°C).
2. Cut the top off the bread and hollow out the center.
3. Place Brie inside the bread bowl and drizzle with honey.
4. Sprinkle with pecans and rosemary.
5. Bake for 20 minutes until cheese is melted.

Spinach and Feta Stuffed Flatbread

Ingredients:

- 2 cups all-purpose flour
- ½ cup Greek yogurt
- ½ tsp baking powder
- 1 cup fresh spinach, chopped
- ½ cup feta cheese, crumbled
- 1 tbsp olive oil

Instructions:

1. In a bowl, mix flour, baking powder, and yogurt to form a dough.
2. Divide into four pieces and roll out into circles.
3. Mix spinach and feta, then place a portion onto one half of each circle.
4. Fold and seal edges, then cook in a pan with olive oil for 3 minutes per side.

Honey Butter Dinner Rolls

Ingredients:

- 3 cups flour
- 1 packet (2 ¼ tsp) yeast
- 1 cup warm milk
- ¼ cup honey
- ¼ cup butter, melted
- 1 egg
- ½ tsp salt

Instructions:

1. In a bowl, combine yeast, warm milk, and honey. Let sit for 5 minutes.
2. Mix in butter, egg, salt, and flour. Knead until smooth.
3. Let dough rise for 1 hour.
4. Divide into 12 rolls, place on a baking sheet, and let rise for 30 minutes.
5. Bake at 375°F (190°C) for 15 minutes.

Pumpkin Spice Bread

Ingredients:

- 1 ¾ cups flour
- 1 tsp baking soda
- ½ tsp salt
- 1 tsp cinnamon
- ½ tsp nutmeg
- ½ tsp ginger
- 1 cup pumpkin puree
- ½ cup sugar
- ½ cup brown sugar
- ½ cup oil
- 2 eggs

Instructions:

1. Preheat oven to 350°F (175°C) and grease a loaf pan.
2. In a bowl, mix flour, baking soda, salt, cinnamon, nutmeg, and ginger.
3. In another bowl, whisk pumpkin, sugars, oil, and eggs.
4. Combine wet and dry ingredients, then pour into the loaf pan.
5. Bake for 50-55 minutes.

Classic Reuben Sandwich

Ingredients:

- 2 slices rye bread
- 4 oz corned beef
- 2 slices Swiss cheese
- ¼ cup sauerkraut
- 2 tbsp Russian dressing
- 1 tbsp butter

Instructions:

1. Butter one side of each slice of bread.
2. Layer corned beef, Swiss cheese, sauerkraut, and Russian dressing between bread slices.
3. Grill in a pan over medium heat for 3-4 minutes per side.

Soft Pretzels with Mustard Dip

Ingredients:

- 3 cups flour
- 1 packet (2 ¼ tsp) yeast
- 1 cup warm water
- 1 tbsp sugar
- 1 tsp salt
- ¼ cup baking soda
- 1 egg, beaten
- Coarse salt

For Mustard Dip:

- ¼ cup Dijon mustard
- 1 tbsp honey

Instructions:

1. Mix yeast, warm water, and sugar. Let sit for 5 minutes.
2. Add flour and salt, knead, and let rise for 1 hour.
3. Divide dough into pieces and roll into ropes. Shape into pretzels.
4. Dip each into a pot of boiling water with baking soda for 30 seconds.
5. Brush with egg wash, sprinkle with salt, and bake at 400°F (200°C) for 12 minutes.

Italian Focaccia with Rosemary

Ingredients:

- 3 cups flour
- 1 packet (2 ¼ tsp) yeast
- 1 cup warm water
- ¼ cup olive oil
- 1 tsp salt
- 2 tbsp fresh rosemary

Instructions:

1. Mix yeast, warm water, and sugar. Let sit for 5 minutes.
2. Add flour, olive oil, and salt, then knead into a dough. Let rise for 1 hour.
3. Spread dough into a greased pan and press with fingers to create dimples.
4. Sprinkle rosemary and drizzle with olive oil.
5. Bake at 375°F (190°C) for 20 minutes.

Croque Monsieur

Ingredients:

- 4 slices white bread
- 4 oz ham
- 2 oz Gruyère cheese, grated
- 2 tbsp butter
- 1 tbsp Dijon mustard
- ½ cup béchamel sauce

Instructions:

1. Preheat oven to 400°F (200°C).
2. Spread Dijon mustard on two slices of bread.
3. Layer ham and Gruyère cheese, then top with the remaining bread slices.
4. Toast sandwiches in butter over medium heat until golden.
5. Transfer to a baking sheet, top with béchamel sauce and extra cheese.
6. Bake for 5 minutes, then broil until bubbly.

Avocado Toast with Poached Egg

Ingredients:

- 2 slices sourdough bread
- 1 ripe avocado
- 2 eggs
- 1 tbsp vinegar
- Salt, pepper, and red pepper flakes

Instructions:

1. Toast bread slices until golden.
2. Mash avocado and spread on toast, seasoning with salt and pepper.
3. Bring a pot of water to a simmer, add vinegar, and poach eggs for 3 minutes.
4. Place eggs on avocado toast, sprinkle with red pepper flakes, and serve.

Savory Herb and Cheese Biscuits

Ingredients:

- 2 cups flour
- 1 tbsp baking powder
- ½ tsp salt
- ½ cup butter, cold and cubed
- 1 cup shredded cheddar cheese
- 2 tbsp fresh herbs (parsley, chives)
- ¾ cup buttermilk

Instructions:

1. Preheat oven to 425°F (220°C).
2. Mix flour, baking powder, and salt.
3. Cut in butter until crumbly, then fold in cheese and herbs.
4. Add buttermilk and mix until dough forms.
5. Roll out and cut biscuits.
6. Bake for 12-15 minutes until golden.

Cuban Sandwich

Ingredients:

- 1 loaf Cuban bread
- 4 oz roast pork
- 4 oz ham
- 4 slices Swiss cheese
- 2 tbsp yellow mustard
- 2 tbsp butter
- 4 pickle slices

Instructions:

1. Slice bread and spread mustard on both halves.
2. Layer ham, roast pork, Swiss cheese, and pickles.
3. Press sandwich in a heated pan with butter, cooking until crispy and cheese is melted.

Sticky Toffee Bread Pudding

Ingredients:

- 4 cups cubed stale bread
- 1 cup heavy cream
- ½ cup milk
- ½ cup brown sugar
- 2 eggs
- 1 tsp vanilla extract
- ½ cup chopped dates

Instructions:

1. Preheat oven to 350°F (175°C).
2. Whisk cream, milk, sugar, eggs, and vanilla.
3. Soak bread cubes in mixture for 15 minutes.
4. Fold in chopped dates and transfer to a baking dish.
5. Bake for 30-35 minutes until set.

New Orleans Beignets

Ingredients:

- 3 ½ cups flour
- ¾ cup warm water
- ¼ cup sugar
- 1 packet (2 ¼ tsp) yeast
- 1 egg
- 2 tbsp butter, melted
- Powdered sugar for dusting

Instructions:

1. Mix yeast, warm water, and sugar. Let sit for 5 minutes.
2. Add egg, butter, and flour, kneading into a dough. Let rise for 1 hour.
3. Roll out dough and cut into squares.
4. Fry in hot oil until golden brown.
5. Dust with powdered sugar before serving.

Classic Bagels with Cream Cheese

Ingredients:

- 4 cups flour
- 1 packet (2 ¼ tsp) yeast
- 1 ½ cups warm water
- 2 tbsp sugar
- 1 tsp salt
- 1 egg (for egg wash)
- 1 tbsp sesame or poppy seeds (optional)
- ½ cup cream cheese

Instructions:

1. Mix yeast, warm water, and sugar. Let sit for 5 minutes.
2. Add flour and salt, knead, and let rise for 1 hour.
3. Shape dough into bagels and boil in water for 1 minute per side.
4. Brush with egg wash and sprinkle seeds if desired.
5. Bake at 375°F (190°C) for 20 minutes.
6. Serve with cream cheese.

Caramelized Onion and Gruyère Tart

Ingredients:

- 1 sheet puff pastry
- 2 large onions, thinly sliced
- 2 tbsp butter
- 1 tsp balsamic vinegar
- 1 cup Gruyère cheese, grated
- 1 egg (for egg wash)

Instructions:

1. Preheat oven to 375°F (190°C).
2. Cook onions in butter until golden, then stir in balsamic vinegar.
3. Roll out puff pastry and layer caramelized onions and cheese on top.
4. Brush edges with egg wash and bake for 20 minutes.

Turkish Pide with Ground Lamb

Ingredients:

- 2 cups flour
- ½ cup warm water
- 1 tsp yeast
- 1 tbsp olive oil
- ½ tsp salt
- ½ lb ground lamb
- ½ onion, chopped
- 1 tsp cumin
- ½ tsp paprika

Instructions:

1. Mix yeast, warm water, and flour to form dough. Let rise for 1 hour.
2. Sauté lamb with onion, cumin, and paprika.
3. Roll out dough into an oval, spread lamb mixture on top, and fold edges slightly.
4. Bake at 375°F (190°C) for 20 minutes.

Garlic Knots with Marinara

Ingredients:

- 2 cups pizza dough
- 2 tbsp butter, melted
- 2 cloves garlic, minced
- 1 tbsp parsley, chopped
- ½ cup marinara sauce

Instructions:

1. Preheat oven to 375°F (190°C).
2. Roll out pizza dough and cut into strips. Tie into knots.
3. Mix butter, garlic, and parsley, then brush over knots.
4. Bake for 15 minutes until golden.
5. Serve with marinara sauce.

Nutella-Stuffed Croissants

Ingredients:

- 1 sheet puff pastry
- ½ cup Nutella
- 1 egg (for egg wash)
- Powdered sugar (for dusting)

Instructions:

1. Preheat oven to 375°F (190°C).
2. Roll out puff pastry and cut into triangles.
3. Place a spoonful of Nutella at the base of each triangle and roll into croissants.
4. Brush with egg wash and bake for 15 minutes.
5. Dust with powdered sugar before serving.

German Soft Pretzel Rolls

Ingredients:

- 4 cups flour
- 1 packet (2 ¼ tsp) yeast
- 1 ½ cups warm water
- 2 tbsp sugar
- 1 tsp salt
- ½ cup baking soda (for boiling)
- Coarse salt (for topping)

Instructions:

1. Mix yeast, warm water, and sugar. Let sit for 5 minutes.
2. Add flour and salt, knead, and let rise for 1 hour.
3. Shape dough into rolls and boil in water with baking soda for 30 seconds.
4. Bake at 375°F (190°C) for 20 minutes.

Challah French Toast

Ingredients:

- 4 slices challah bread
- 2 eggs
- ½ cup milk
- 1 tsp cinnamon
- 1 tbsp sugar
- 1 tsp vanilla extract
- Butter for frying
- Maple syrup (for serving)

Instructions:

1. Whisk eggs, milk, cinnamon, sugar, and vanilla.
2. Dip challah slices in mixture and let soak for 30 seconds.
3. Cook in butter over medium heat until golden.
4. Serve with maple syrup.

Classic BLT Sandwich

Ingredients:

- 2 slices sandwich bread
- 4 slices bacon, cooked
- 2 lettuce leaves
- 2 tomato slices
- 2 tbsp mayonnaise

Instructions:

1. Toast bread slices.
2. Spread mayonnaise on each slice.
3. Layer bacon, lettuce, and tomato.
4. Close sandwich and serve.

Spicy Buffalo Chicken Sliders

Ingredients:

- 6 slider buns
- 1 cup shredded cooked chicken
- ¼ cup buffalo sauce
- ¼ cup ranch dressing
- 6 pickle slices

Instructions:

1. Mix shredded chicken with buffalo sauce.
2. Place chicken on slider buns and drizzle with ranch dressing.
3. Add pickle slices and serve.

Irish Soda Bread

Ingredients:

- 4 cups flour
- 1 tsp baking soda
- 1 tsp salt
- 1 ¾ cups buttermilk

Instructions:

1. Preheat oven to 375°F (190°C).
2. Mix flour, baking soda, and salt.
3. Add buttermilk and mix until dough forms.
4. Shape into a round loaf and bake for 35 minutes.

Ham and Cheese Croissant Sandwich

Ingredients:

- 2 croissants, sliced
- 4 oz ham
- 2 slices Swiss cheese
- 2 tbsp Dijon mustard

Instructions:

1. Preheat oven to 350°F (175°C).
2. Spread Dijon mustard on croissant halves.
3. Layer ham and cheese, then close croissants.
4. Bake for 10 minutes until cheese melts.

Baguette with Olive Tapenade

Ingredients:

- 1 French baguette
- ½ cup black olives, chopped
- 2 tbsp capers
- 1 tbsp olive oil
- 1 tsp lemon juice
- 1 garlic clove, minced

Instructions:

1. Mix olives, capers, olive oil, lemon juice, and garlic.
2. Slice baguette and spread tapenade on top.

Cinnamon Raisin Bagels

Ingredients:

- 4 cups flour
- 1 packet (2 ¼ tsp) yeast
- 1 ½ cups warm water
- 2 tbsp sugar
- 1 tsp cinnamon
- ½ cup raisins
- 1 egg (for egg wash)

Instructions:

1. Mix yeast, warm water, and sugar. Let sit for 5 minutes.
2. Add flour, cinnamon, and raisins, knead, and let rise for 1 hour.
3. Shape dough into bagels and boil in water for 1 minute per side.
4. Brush with egg wash and bake at 375°F (190°C) for 20 minutes.

Spinach and Artichoke Dip with Bread Bowl

Ingredients:

- 1 round loaf bread
- 1 cup spinach, chopped
- 1 cup artichoke hearts, chopped
- 1 cup cream cheese
- ½ cup sour cream
- ½ cup grated Parmesan
- ½ tsp garlic powder

Instructions:

1. Preheat oven to 375°F (190°C).
2. Mix spinach, artichokes, cream cheese, sour cream, Parmesan, and garlic powder.
3. Cut top off bread and hollow out center.
4. Fill with spinach dip and bake for 20 minutes.

Tomato and Mozzarella Panini

Ingredients:

- 2 ciabatta rolls
- 4 slices fresh mozzarella
- 1 tomato, sliced
- 4 fresh basil leaves
- 2 tbsp pesto
- 1 tbsp olive oil

Instructions:

1. Preheat a panini press or skillet over medium heat.
2. Slice ciabatta rolls and spread pesto on each side.
3. Layer mozzarella, tomato slices, and basil leaves.
4. Drizzle with olive oil and close the sandwich.
5. Grill for 3–5 minutes until golden brown and cheese is melted.

Prosciutto and Fig Flatbread

Ingredients:

- 1 flatbread
- 4 slices prosciutto
- ½ cup fresh figs, sliced
- ½ cup goat cheese
- 1 tbsp honey
- 1 tbsp balsamic glaze

Instructions:

1. Preheat oven to 375°F (190°C).
2. Place flatbread on a baking sheet and top with goat cheese, prosciutto, and figs.
3. Drizzle with honey and bake for 10 minutes.
4. Remove from oven, drizzle with balsamic glaze, and serve.

Texas Toast with Herb Butter

Ingredients:

- 4 thick slices of bread
- ½ cup butter, softened
- 2 cloves garlic, minced
- 1 tbsp fresh parsley, chopped
- ½ tsp salt

Instructions:

1. Mix butter, garlic, parsley, and salt.
2. Spread mixture on both sides of bread slices.
3. Cook on a skillet over medium heat for 2 minutes per side until golden brown.

Classic Philly Cheesesteak

Ingredients:

- 1 hoagie roll
- ½ lb ribeye steak, thinly sliced
- ½ cup onions, sliced
- ½ cup green bell peppers, sliced
- 2 slices provolone cheese
- 1 tbsp olive oil

Instructions:

1. Heat olive oil in a skillet over medium-high heat.
2. Sauté onions and bell peppers until soft.
3. Add sliced steak and cook until browned.
4. Place cheese slices over the steak until melted.
5. Fill hoagie roll with the mixture and serve.

Chocolate Chip Banana Muffins

Ingredients:

- 2 ripe bananas, mashed
- 1 ½ cups flour
- ½ cup sugar
- 1 tsp baking soda
- ½ tsp salt
- ½ cup butter, melted
- 1 egg
- ½ cup chocolate chips

Instructions:

1. Preheat oven to 350°F (175°C).
2. Mix flour, sugar, baking soda, and salt.
3. In another bowl, combine mashed bananas, butter, and egg.
4. Mix wet and dry ingredients, then fold in chocolate chips.
5. Spoon batter into muffin tin and bake for 20 minutes.

Cornbread with Honey Butter

Ingredients:

- 1 cup cornmeal
- 1 cup flour
- ½ cup sugar
- 1 tsp baking powder
- 1 cup buttermilk
- 1 egg
- ½ cup butter, melted
- ¼ cup honey (for honey butter)

Instructions:

1. Preheat oven to 375°F (190°C).
2. Mix cornmeal, flour, sugar, and baking powder.
3. Add buttermilk, egg, and melted butter.
4. Pour into a greased baking dish and bake for 20 minutes.
5. Mix honey with butter and spread on warm cornbread.

Apple Cinnamon Bread

Ingredients:

- 2 cups flour
- 1 cup sugar
- 1 tsp baking soda
- 1 tsp cinnamon
- ½ tsp salt
- 2 apples, diced
- 2 eggs
- ½ cup vegetable oil

Instructions:

1. Preheat oven to 350°F (175°C).
2. Mix flour, sugar, baking soda, cinnamon, and salt.
3. Add eggs and oil, then fold in apples.
4. Pour batter into a loaf pan and bake for 50 minutes.

French Baguette with Brie and Jam

Ingredients:

- 1 French baguette
- 4 oz brie cheese
- ¼ cup raspberry jam
- 1 tbsp honey

Instructions:

1. Slice baguette and spread brie cheese on each slice.
2. Top with raspberry jam and drizzle with honey.

Meatball Sub Sandwich

Ingredients:

- 1 sub roll
- 4 meatballs
- ½ cup marinara sauce
- 2 slices provolone cheese
- 1 tbsp butter

Instructions:

1. Heat meatballs in marinara sauce.
2. Toast sub roll with butter in a skillet.
3. Place meatballs inside the roll, top with cheese, and broil for 3 minutes.

Olive and Parmesan Focaccia

Ingredients:

- 2 cups flour
- 1 packet (2 ¼ tsp) yeast
- ¾ cup warm water
- 1 tsp salt
- 2 tbsp olive oil
- ½ cup black olives, sliced
- ¼ cup Parmesan cheese

Instructions:

1. Mix yeast, warm water, and flour. Let sit for 10 minutes.
2. Add salt and olive oil, knead dough, and let rise for 1 hour.
3. Spread onto a baking sheet, top with olives and Parmesan.
4. Bake at 375°F (190°C) for 20 minutes.

Cheesy Bacon Breadsticks

Ingredients:

- 1 pizza dough
- ½ cup mozzarella cheese, shredded
- 4 slices bacon, crumbled
- 2 tbsp butter, melted

Instructions:

1. Preheat oven to 375°F (190°C).
2. Roll out pizza dough and brush with melted butter.
3. Sprinkle mozzarella cheese and bacon.
4. Slice into strips and bake for 12–15 minutes.

www.ingramcontent.com/pod-product-compliance
Lightning Source LLC
LaVergne TN
LVHW061953070526
838199LV00060B/4097